BURPOZADE

the ENERGY DRINK FOR ATHLETES

£3.10

Printed and Published in Great Britain
by D. C. Thomson & Co., Ltd.,
185 Fleet Street, London, EC4A 2HS.

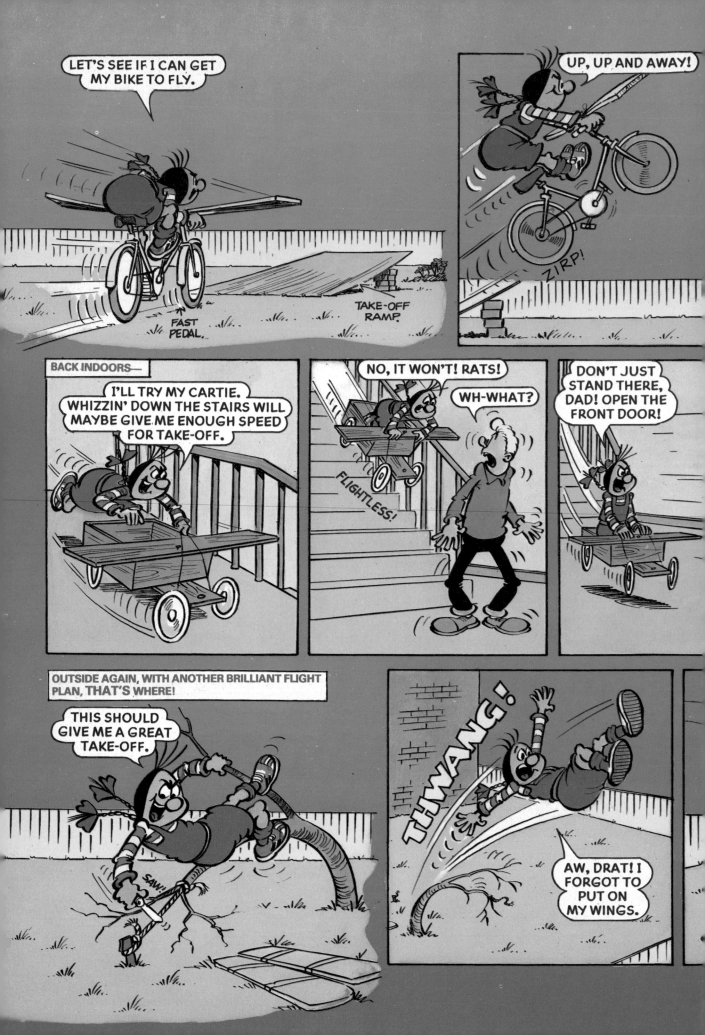

FLIGHTS of FANCY!

(NUTTY FLYING NOTIONS OF LONG AGO.)

A Persian king once thought that by tying four eagles to his throne he could fly. He was to guide the eagles by holding a piece of meat in front of them. Fortunately for him, he never tried the idea!

In the 18th century, a Portuguese friar, Barthelemy-Laurent de Guzman, claimed that he could make a machine that would fly by magnetism.

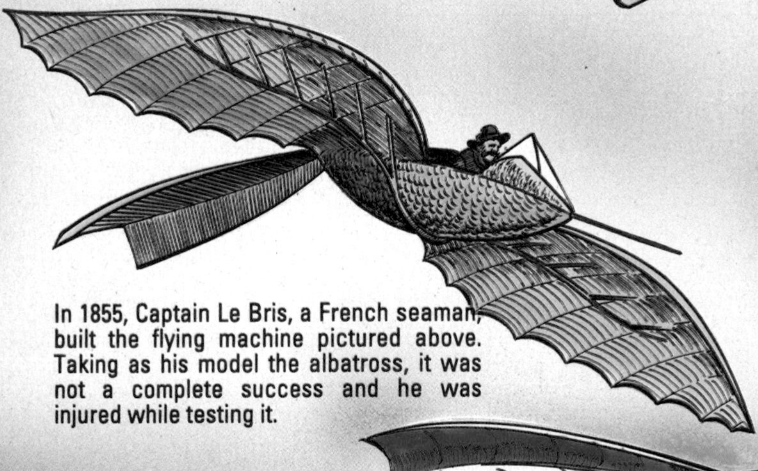

In 1855, Captain Le Bris, a French seaman, built the flying machine pictured above. Taking as his model the albatross, it was not a complete success and he was injured while testing it.

Possibly the earliest idea man had for a flying machine was a large pair of wings which were attached to the arms and flapped like those of a bird.

Leonardo da Vinci, the famous fifteenth-century scientist and engineer, designed this glider. There is no record that he ever tried to fly it.

This astonishing airship was build in 1834 by a Frenchman, Comte de Lennox. It was to be rowed through the air, but proved too heavy to rise from the ground.

A Jesuit priest, Francesco Lana, designed this odd aerial ship in 1670. The four copper balls were to have all the air removed from them to provide the lifting power.

In Vienna in 1809, Jacob Degen gave up his trade as a watchmaker to build this remarkable winged machine, to be worked by arm power.

Besnier, a locksmith of Sablé, France, made this peculiar gliding machine in 1678. The flaps opened on the down-stroke and closed on the upstroke.

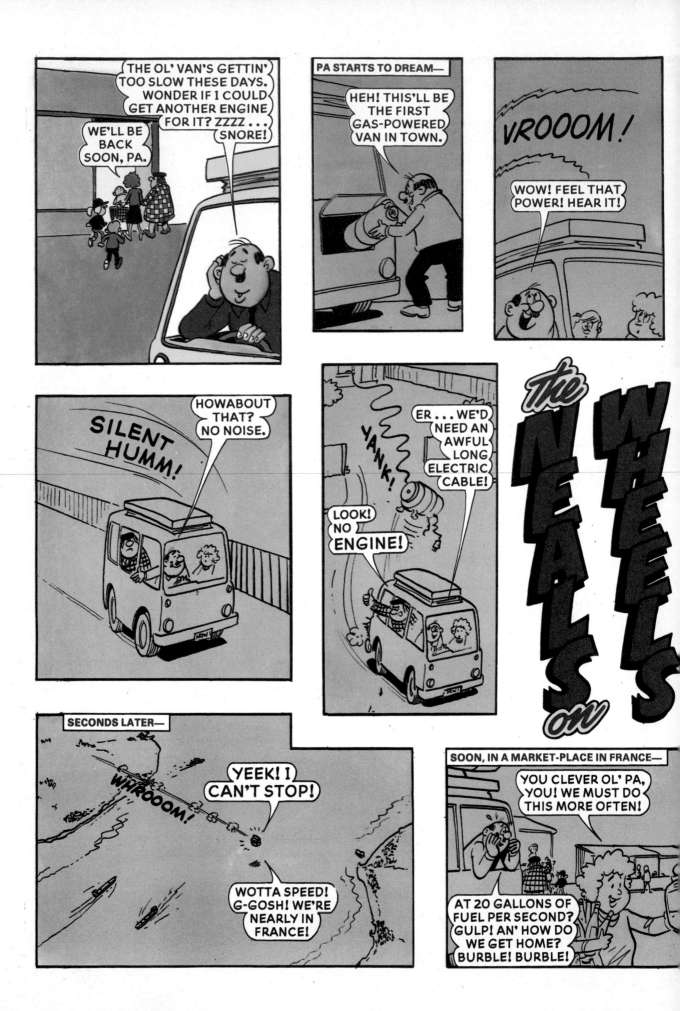

EARLY TRANSPORT

BY OUR TALL-TALE CORRESPONDENT.

'INTERNAL COMBUSTION' ENGINE

Improving upon experiments made by earlier inventors — notably G. Fawkes, Esq. — the designer of this machine was last seen on the first and only day of its public demonstration. It took off — and so did its inventor.

ONE-HORSE-POWER CAR

This invention, a fine example of early Victorian genius — as clever as the backward-firing musket — made rapid strides. But, alas, it, too, was doomed to failure when an oats shortage drove prices up. Despite the cheapness of the recently discovered petroleum, the one-horse-power car ended up on the scrap heap. Neither horse nor driver could stomach the new fiery drink.

EARLY EXTERNAL COMBUSTION ENGINE

This was a huge success — until the balloon-blowers (or WALLIES as they were nicknamed) went on strike for danger money. The inventors couldn't raise the wind and the engine soon became a museum piece.

SAIL-CAR

This was invented for use by retired sea captains and ancient mariners. But the Sail-Car never really fulfilled its inventor's dreams. Calm days were a wash-out, and the braking system was a nightmare — especially for passers-by. Sails — er — sales quickly dropped off.

PEOPLE'S CAR

After many years of research and months of development, D. Decker, the inventor, finally got his car on the road. An instant success, the People's Car was soon to be seen rattling all over Britain during the summer of 1825. Then a rival, a Mister George Stephenson, appeared on the scene with the loco idea of putting coaches on rails and pulling them along behind singing kettles! Sales of the People's Car suddenly hit the buffers.

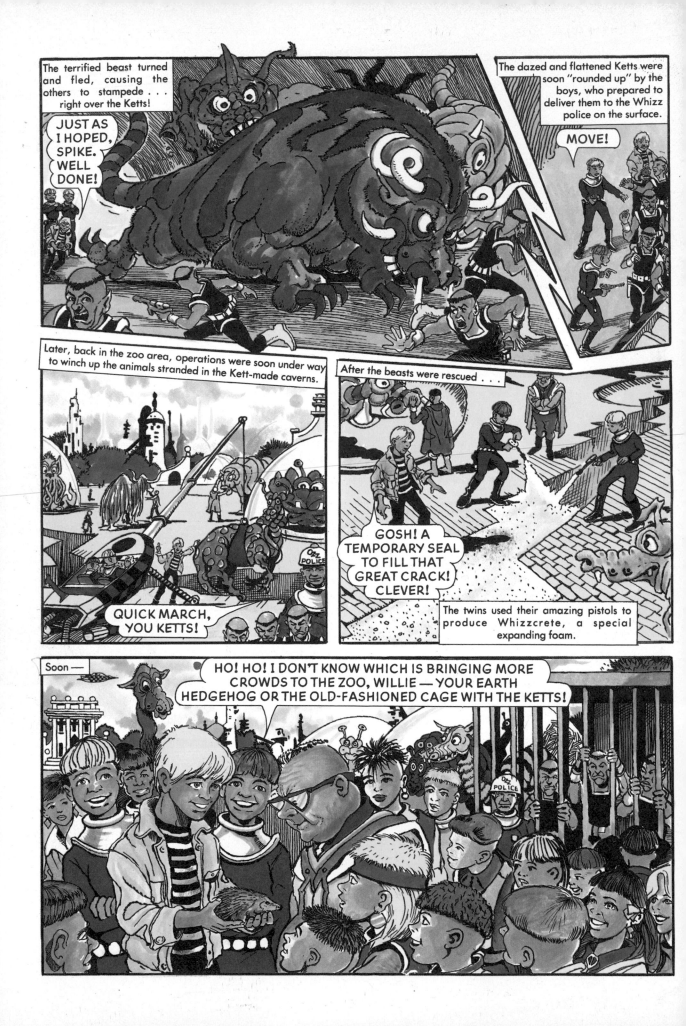

ALL CHANGE!

SOME YOUNGSTERS WHO *DON'T* LOOK LIKE MUM OR DAD!

Although adult LIONS have no spots, young lion cubs are so spotted that they can almost be mistaken for young leopards. The spots disappear long before the cubs are fully-grown.

Certain LANGURS in the forests of Borneo are coloured black and white. But their young ones' glossy-black hair does not grow in until they are older.

A young PENGUIN seems more like an animal than a bird because of its coat of downy feathers which looks so furry. The youngster soon appears bigger than its parents because of the bulky "fur coat".

Fully-grown MALAYAN TAPIRS are black and white in colour, with no stripes or spots. But their young ones are marked with both stripes and spots.

Here you see a ROE DEER with its young, known as fawns. The youngster is spotted all over its body. These spots act as a sort of "camouflage", making it difficult to see the young animal in woodland thickets.

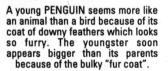

Here you can see how the young ALLIGATORS from the swamps of the Mississippi River, in America, differ from their parents. All the youngsters are striped on the underside. The adult alligators have no stripes.

When young EMUS are hatched, they have spotted legs and striped backs. The spots disappear from their legs within a few days, but the stripes can be clearly seen until the birds are more than half-grown.

This funny little BROWN LEMUR has patches of black and white fur on its face, but as you can see there is no trace of these patches on its mother's face.

The GANNET or SOLAN GOOSE hatches its young on rocks and cliff-edges near the sea-coast. At first the young gannets are covered with fluffy, white down. Later, their plumage becomes thickly speckled, but the adult birds have no speckles at all.

Young SWANS, known as cygnets, are covered with light-brown downy feathers. The brown feathers disappear slowly as the young swans grow, but the birds are nearly full-grown before the plumage becomes all white.

Over its nostrils a fully-grown HOODED SEAL has a strange bladder of skin which it is able to blow up with air to frighten enemies. Young seals are lighter-coloured, and do not have this bladder until they are fully-grown.

Young Indian WILD PIGS have clearly-marked stripes on their backs. The stripes, which fade gradually as the pigs grow older, eventually disappear.

The RAZOR-BILL is a common sea bird on some parts of the British coast. The young, apart from having downy feathers, are also different from grown-up birds because their heads are white, instead of black.

South American LLAMAS are used for carrying loads in mountainous country. As you can see, the older beast is covered with long, shaggy hair, while the young llama's coat is much shorter and of a different colour.

Baby PUMAS have fur of a lighter colour than their parents, and are covered with black spots. The spots disappear as the cub grows up.

The African ELAND, a very large antelope, has no stripes on its coat. Yet across their backs, young elands have narrow light-coloured stripes which disappear as they grow older.

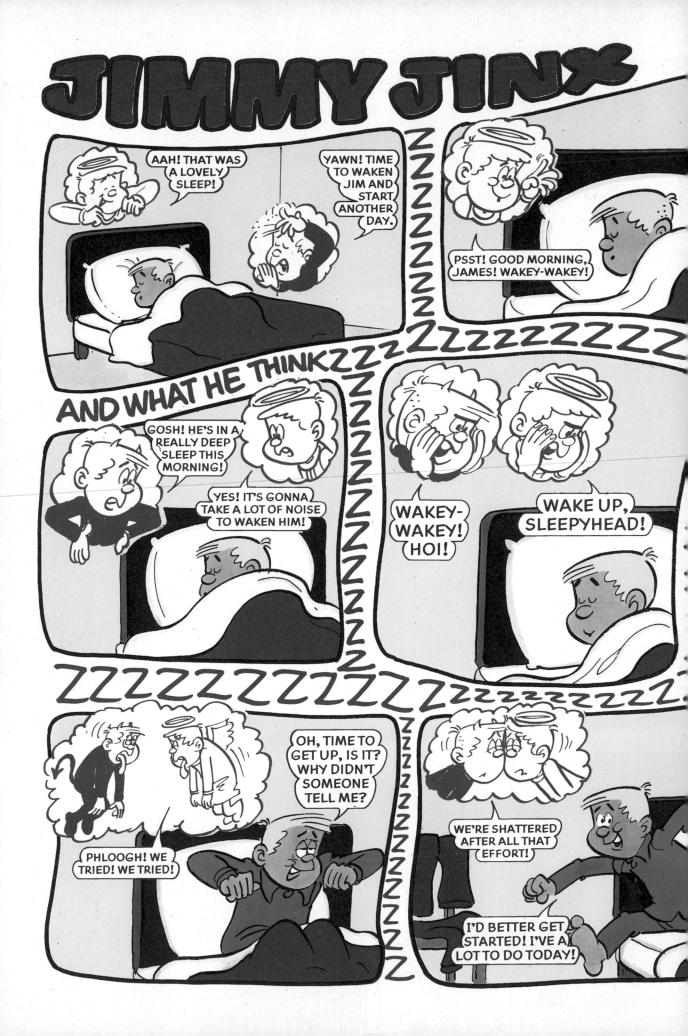

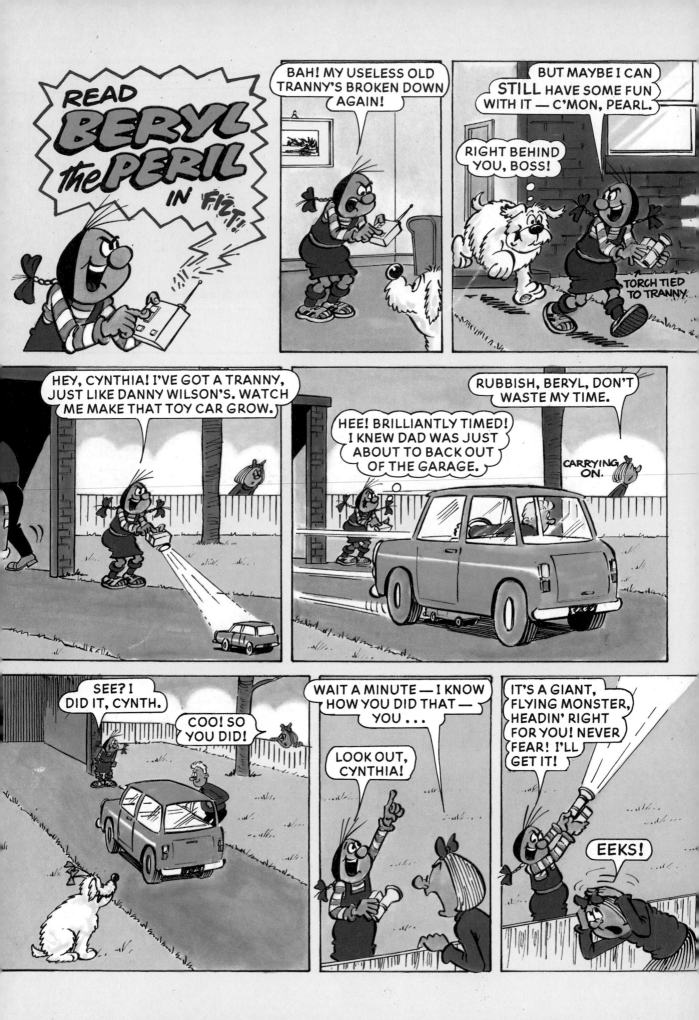